WARSAW

past and present

Anna Kotańska
Anna Topolska

 Wydawnictwo PARMA® PRESS

WARSAW

past and present

Nowhere in Europe is there a capital city as tragically afflicted by history as the one lying close to the continent's heart, the Polish capital of Warsaw. But as he or she strolls along the narrow streets of that city's Old and New Towns, or admires the historic buildings along its Royal Way, the visitor may never now realise that just around half a century ago all of this lay in almost total ruin.

Warsaw – the former seat of the Dukes of Mazovia and place of election of the Kings of Poland – has been the country's capital since 1596. Indeed, it has shared the fate of the nation for even longer – for seven centuries now, being the venue for many of the most outstanding and dramatic events. However, of all those centuries, it was perhaps the 20th that turned out to be the most resounding in its impact. Within just the last one hundred years what was a provincial city within the Russian Empire became once again the capital of a newly reborn Poland has been devastated once and twice been witness to the rebirth of the state of which it is capital.

Polish independence in the years immediately after the First World War led to rapid progress in making up for the time lost during the awful period of Poland's partitioning between the Russian, Prussian and Austrian empires. During the Second World War was almost completely annihilated. However, thanks to the exceptional determination of Varsovians, it was rebuilt and today the city is a European metropolis once again.

And it is this, the 20th century fate of Warsaw, that we are able to present here on the basis of archival photographs from the collections of the Historical Museum of Warsaw, as well as a comparison with the contemporary photographic work of Christian Parma.

a capital reborn

Warsaw entered the 20th century as a city in the Russian-partitioned part of Poland with a population of 700,000 inhabitants but, being limited in territorial extent by the fortifications and buildings of the Russian garrison, it covered just 34.5 km². Signs of foreign occupation and domination were visible at every step. Alongside the military patrols and dual-language notices, the most eyecatching elements were the Orthodox churches and other buildings remodelled in the "Russian" style. The Royal Castle – symbol of Poland's past majesty – had become the seat of the Tsar's Governors-General, while the residence of Poland's last King, Stanisław August Poniatowski, in Łazienki Park, had fallen into the hands of the Romanovs. Other fine Warsaw palaces were occupied by the Russians as offices.

From among the ranks of the Tsarist officials, the only one to have earned a more affectionate place in the memory of Varsovians is city president Sokrates Starynkiewicz, thanks to whom a series of important developments were launched and pursued – notably the installation of water mains and sewers, the bringing into operation of telephones and horse-drawn trams and the linking-up of some of the suburbs. Warsaw, whose development had been confined with pre-meditation by the St. Petersburg authorities, was now able to change its face gradually. New streets (like Służewska, Chopina and Moniuszki) were laid out, and existing ones modernised or lengthened (as with Jasna and Targowa). New architecturally – or functionally-interesting buildings went up, notably Zachęta - the headquarters of the Society for the Cultivation of the Fine Arts, the Philharmonic Hall, Warsaw University Library, the Polytechnic, Dom Techników (seat of the Technicians' Association), and such churches as St. Florian's and St. Augustine's. Transport links were improved through the building of the "Third Bridge" (now named after Poniatowski), as well as the railway bridge near the Citadel. The newly-erected structures were all representative of the most up-to-date trends in the architecture of their day.

The First World War years were a time of dramatic events for Warsaw, as well as of political and social change. Retreating in disarray on August 5th 1915, the Russian forces burnt railway stations, blew up bridges and ransacked the city as a whole. The entry of the German forces was accepted without enthusiasm, but their occupation was characterised by a reviving of domestic politics, and a certain freedom in that part of life concerning culture. Thus, the Polish University and Polytechnic were reactivated in 1915, and the commemoration of the 125th anniversary of the enactment of the May 3rd Constitution offered a tangible piece of evidence of the change. A Polish Kingdom was proclaimed on November 5th 1916, but the attitude of the Germans was to consider the Polish lands conquered territory absolutely open to all forms of exploitation. Industries, finances and commerce collapsed as a result. Nevertheless, the situation at the Front fostered an increasing radicalism among Poles that ultimately led to the Germans on Warsaw streets being disarmed. November 11th 1918 saw Poland regain its independence after 123 years of partitions. Warsaw was again the capital city.

Alas, as early as in 1919, the existence of the free Polish state was to come under threat from a westward encroachment by the Red Army. As its commander said: "the road to worldwide conflagration runs across Poland's corpse". By August 1920, the Bolsheviks were on the outskirts of Warsaw. However, on August 15th, the Polish armed forces under the command of Józef Piłsudski held the invader in the battle at Ossów and Radzymin known as the "Miracle on the Vistula", which prevented the forces of communism from flooding across Europe.

As the external threat diminished, Varsovians were at last able to deal with the business of the city. Their entrepreneurship and energy was to bear fruit rapidly, with Warsaw entering a period of dynamic development and making up for the time lost through the period of Partitions. The country's political, economic and cultural life concentrated in its capital, while the most important national authorities, central offices, scientific and artistic institutions also set up here. In addition, Warsaw took up the role of important industrial centre and main transport node of Poland.

In connection with all this, the capital drew in a steady influx of new inhabitants, such that the 20 years between the Wars saw the population rise by over 500,000 to 1.3 million. In the face of a consequent ballooning in the demand for housing, estates of apartment blocks appeared (like those of the Warsaw Housing Cooperative and Society of Workers' Estates), along with more exclusive housing (in Żoliborz, Ochota and Mokotów districts) that often recalled the old Polish manors of the nobility, or modern villas (as, i.a. in Saska Kępa). In the Śródmieście district in particular, single new houses nicknamed "fillings"appeared. Work was also done to give Warsaw better public buildings, mostly Modernist in style, including the Parliament Building, Ministry of Communications and headquarters of ZUS (the National Insurance Agency). The seats of financial institutions (like the National Holding Bank and the State Agricultural Bank) went up, as did those of such scientific institutions as the Geological Institute, such educational establishments as the Higher School of Commerce (today's Warsaw School of Economics), the Academy of Physical Education and Polytechnic, and such cultural institutions as the National Museum. A great many commercial premises were also erected. However, in no sense did all this new building leave the Warsaw heritage destroyed or degraded by the Partitioners forgotten. Much attention was in fact paid to restoration work, among other things of the Royal Castle, Staszic Palace and tenement houses of the Old Town Market Square. And the development went on: a river port was worked on, a cross-city rail-link, extensions and widening work on the main transport routes, the laying out of new streets, and the bringing into order of land along the Vistula.

An undoubted attraction of the capital was the wealth of artistic and cultural events it could offer. The Opera House (Grand Theatre), National Theatre and Mały and Nowy Theatres could accommodate an extensive repertoire that ranged from the great classics to enthusiastically-received cabaret performances and reviews. The several tens of cinemas were the place to see Polish films above all, though foreign movies also made their appearance. The radio was hugely popular from the moment it went on the air in 1925, and an Experimental Television Station was up and running as early as in 1938. Put in place immediately in 1918, the Polska Agencja Telegraficzna offered the numerous Warsaw newspaper titles a wide-ranging information service regularly updated. The literary circles in turn centred around the greatest writers of the day (like Stefan Żeromski, Zofia Nałkowska, Andrzej Strug and Maria Dąbrowska). Poets came together within the Skamander group, which included Julian Tuwim, Kazimierz Wierzyński, Jan Lechoń, Jarosław Iwaszkiewicz and Antoni Słonimski. The National Museum, Institute for the Promotion of Art, Polish Artists' Club and many private salons played host to Polish and foreign art, while a real renaissance in graphic art was led by Władysław Skoczylas, Edmund Bartłomiejczyk, Stanisław Ostoja-Chrostowski and others.

An exceptional role in Warsaw's history was that played by its last President before the War, Stefan Starzyński. An excellent manager, organiser and creator of bold solutions, Starzyński sought to raise the prestige of Warsaw as capital of the Second Republic. His plans took in, not only the spatial development of the city, but also fundamental aesthetic changes to it. The scale of these could be seen in a presentation of the future capital at a great exhibition staged at the National Museum in 1938, under the title Warszawa wczoraj, dziś, jutro ("Warsaw Yesterday, Today and Tomorrow". This attracted more than half a million visitors.

* December 1900, and rooms in the Town Hall present Warsaw's first exhibition of post cards. Its 60,000 exhibits attract 16,000 visitors.

* The inaugural concert in the newly-built Philharmonic Hall takes place on November 5th 1901, with the participation of outstanding Polish pianist Ignacy Jan Paderewski; Artur Rubinstein makes his debut here the following year.

* A huge but peaceful demonstration of Polish national identity is the National March in Warsaw held on November 5th 1905 and attended by nearly 200,000 people.

* Electric street lighting begins to appear in the city in 1906.

* By 1908, electric trams are operating along some 10-20 city routes, though buses will not appear until 1920.

* Visiting in 1909, French actress Sarah Bernhardt receives the plaudits of Warsaw society.

* Poland's first aircraft manufacturer, "Aviata", goes into production in 1911.

* In May 1912, the whole city seems to turn out for the funeral of Warsaw's most famous chronicler, the much-admired writer and publicist Bolesław Prus.

* December 1927, and Poland's first electrified rail line links the capital with Grodzisk Mazowiecki.

* Every five years from 1927 onwards, Warsaw has played host to the Fryderyk Chopin International Piano Competition. It remains one of the world's most important musical events.

* 1928 sees Varsovians following with great interest the progress with restoring the colourful polychromy to the facades of tenement houses on the Old Town Market Square.

* Height-of-fashion dancing in Warsaw: guests are drawn to the "Adria" restaurant – opened in 1929 – by its revolving dancefloor and mirror-ball and ... by the most fetching of "taxi dancers".

* Europe's most powerful radio station starts up in Raszyn near Warsaw in 1931.

* 1932 brings the opening of the Radium Institute (today's Oncological Institute) in Wawelska Street, at the initiative of Maria Skłodowska-Curie, twice winner of the Nobel Prize and honorary citizen of Warsaw.

* Ballooning competitions for the Gordon Bennett Cup are held twice at Warsaw airport, in 1934 and 1935.

* May 17th 1935: A crowd many thousands strong bids a ceremonial farewell to Marshal Józef Piłsudski, who is laid to rest alongside Poland's Kings on the Wawel Hill in Kraków.

* The Museum of Old Warsaw comes into being in 1936 – as a predecessor of today's the Historical Museum of Warsaw.

* The Legia Stadium notes a record attendance of 40,000 spectators for a 1936 match between Germany and Poland.

* The event of 1938 is the great exhibition entitled Warsaw Yesterday, Today and Tomorrow", presenting achievements to date and future plans for the capital of the Second Polish Republic, as organized in the new National Museum building on Aleje Jerozolimskie.

Part of the view of left-bank Warsaw in 1905 – as seen from Praga District.
In the foreground, part of the built-up area of Praga and the Kierbedź Bridge dating back to 1864.
Post World War II, the bridge was rebuilt – without its characteristic
trusses – as the Śląsko-Dąbrowski Bridge completed 1949.

Zamek - Kolumna Zygmunta III.

The Royal Castle and Zygmunt III Column in Castle Square – a view from before World War I. The old castle of Poland's Kings was the seat of the Tsar's Governors during the years of the Partitions. The country's regaining of independence in 1918 saw the Castle take on a new role as residence of the President of Poland.

Marszałkowska Street around 1912 – as seen from the Zbawiciela (Saviour's) Church side. The photograph presents the kind of buildings typical for the centre of the old Warsaw and now no longer in existence. Pre World War II, this main and most busy street in the city held the headquarters of many well-known firms and banks, as well as elegant shops, cinemas and restaurants.

Brzozowa Street – as seen from the direction of the New Town. This photograph from before the First World War does a good job of encapsulating the overall character and climate of the then Old Town – since the beginning of the 19th century this had been a peripheral and run-down part of Warsaw, above all inhabited by small-time traders, artisans and servants.

A Market in the Old Town Market Square. The marketplace remained here until 1912, when the Society for the Care of the Monuments of the Past took steps to restore the elegance to this historic part of the city, among other things through a remodelling of the Statue of the Mermaid and the resurfacing of the Square.

Part of the elevation of the Pod Orłem ("Sign of the Eagle") tenement house at 18 Piwna Street, inter-War period. Above the door of the tenement house dating from 1718, alongside the old shield with the crowned eagle are shields of artisans' workshops. The Old Town tenement houses were often disfigured by these kinds of plaques and inscriptions quite in contrast with priceless architectural details.

Targowa ul. na Pradze. - Rue Targowa à Praga.

Targowa Street, around 1908-1910. Praga – the right-bank part of Warsaw – was incorporated into the capital city as early as in 1791, but was perceived for at least a hundred years afterwards as separate from the rest, as a poor suburb of limited interest. However, in the late 19th and early 20th centuries the district's main thoroughfare – Targowa Street – changed its appearance: the old marketplaces gave way to a large square, and a wide road was laid out.

16

A bird's-eye view of Saski Square from 1919. To be seen in the foreground is the Saski Garden and Saski Palace no longer in existence. The Square was then dominated by the St. Alexander Nevsky Orthodox Cathedral, which was erected before World War I as a symbol of Russian pre-eminence in Warsaw. This giant building with its golden domes and huge belltower was completely alien in character from the rest of the city's architecture, and was taken down shortly after Poland regained its independence.

World War I – the march of Russian forces out of Warsaw on August 4th 1915. The victorious offensive of the central powers on the Eastern Front led to the enforced expulsion of the Russian army from Warsaw after 100 years of occupation. The withdrawing forces took factory equipment away with them, blew up bridges and generally ravaged the entire Kingdom of Poland.

The National March of May 3rd 1916 – as seen at Trzech Krzyży Square. Taking their lead from a softening of policy towards Poles and the winning of support for them by the Central Powers, the occupying German authorities permitted celebration of the 125th anniversary of the enactment of the May 3rd Constitution (the second in Europe after the French). Around 250,000 Warsaw inhabitants took part in this display of patriotism.

The Saski Garden, c. 1919. A view of part of the main avenue in the garden established by King August II near the Saski Palace. This was Warsaw's first public park, open from 1723 on.

Plac Żelaznej Bramy ("Iron Gate" Square) in the 1930s. One of the busiest parts of old Warsaw was the famous "Za Żelazną Bramą" marketplace. It was possible to buy just about everything in the large market hall with its characteristic arcade, at the stalls around the Lubomirski Palace and in the neighbouring Mirów Hall. This area changed its character entirely after World War II, as the kind of construction visible on the photograph gave way to housing estates 1960s-style.

Mianowskiego Street – the Lubeckiego Estate in 1929. The inter-War period saw many new residential districts go up in Warsaw. These included the ones in Ochota district (the Lubeckiego and Staszica estates), Żoliborz (the so-called "Officers' and Civil Service Żoliborz"), Mokotów and Saska Kępa. Some of these were kept up in the then-fashionable "manorial style".

The "May Subversion" of 1926 – Marshal Józef Piłsudski on the Poniatowski Bridge, surrounded by the military commanders loyal to him. On May 12th 1926, Marshal Piłsudski stood at the head of a military coup staged against the Government of Prime Minister Wincenty Witos. After a three-day struggle, Piłsudski took power, setting up a new government and assigning the function of President to Ignacy Mościcki.

Fot. E. Garda

Warschau, Hochhaus am Postplatz
Warszawa, „Drapacz" przy Pl. Pocztowym
479

Napoleon Square in the 1930s. The turn-of-the-century division into plots of what had been hospital land changed the view of central Warsaw markedly. Today's Plac Powstańców Warszawy (Warsaw Uprisers' Square) – known in 1921 as Napoleon Square – was the site for the building of elegant multi-storey tenement houses, while a square was laid out. Warsaw's first "skyscraper" appeared here in 1933, in the shape of the Prudential Insurance headquarters.

The junction of Zgoda and Szpitalna Streets in the 1930s. This was one of the busiest points in the old city centre, where Bracka, Zgoda, Szpitalna and Chmielna Streets converged. Representative offices of foreign firms located here, as did editorial offices, small theatres, other places of entertainment and elegant shops.

Nowy Świat Street as seen from Krakowskie Przedmieście Street in 1935. This atmospheric photograph of a place loved by Varsovians gives a very good feeling of how things were in the capital between the Wars. The Second Republic brought rapid changes that transformed Warsaw into a modern city.

A Warsaw street in the 1930s. While Warsaw had just over 700,000 people in 1918 it took only 20 years for the number to rise to 1,289,000. For comparison, Stockholm had around half a million people at the time and Vienna c. 1.8 million.

The Bernardine Church in Czerniaków, 1938. The Church of St. Anthony of Padua was erected
at the end of the 17th century to a design from Tylman of Gameren, and was thus one of the finest monuments
linking up with the times of King Jan III Sobieski. The photograph shows part of the rich interior
with its Baroque-style stucco-work and frescoes.

A room in the Przeździecki Palace in Foksal Street as it looked in the 1930s. An example of an original interior of one of Warsaw's aristocratic residences, which were often hired out to diplomats by the owners. Thus the palace of the Branicki family in Frascati Street housed the French Embassy, while the Czapski Palace in Krakowskie Przedmieście was home to the American Ambassador.

A Picnic in Bielany, 1936. Bielany was a favourite place for rest and recreation over many generations. Whitsun was celebrated in the traditional way at the Camaldolese Church and Monastery, with picnics and May excursions being organised. A further attraction was the then extremely popular steamboat cruises that headed for picturesque sections of the Vistula Escarpment.

A charabanc of the Poltur Company around 1939. The inter-War years saw the capital attracting many visitors year after year. The servicing of this tourist traffic was a job for the professional travel agents like "Orbis", "Francopol", "Argos" or "Icar". Bus trips to Warsaw and its environs were in turn a speciality of the Poltur Company, which operated under the patronage of the Polish Sightseeing Society.

the apocalypse

The outbreak of World War II on September 1st 1939 put paid to the great opportunity that Warsaw had seemed to have – under City President Starzyński's administration – to become a metropolis on the European scale. During the tragic days of the siege of Warsaw, Starzyński came on the radio to say that: "I wanted Warsaw to be great. I believed it would be great. My associates and I drew up plans and made sketches of a great Warsaw of the future." But instead of a role putting this bold urban plan into action, Starzyński found himself heading the city's civil defence in support of the army. Warsaw was under German attack from day one of the War, and there was no let up to the air raids and artillery bombardments that were ultimately to come to a head on September 25th. In the face of the aggressor's military superiority and the tragic conditions in which inhabitants found themselves, the besieged capital had no option but to capitulate on September 28th. 30,000 had died in its defence, with more than 50,000 wounded. Many residential and public buildings had been damaged (all the hospitals, for example), along with such monuments as the Royal Castle, St. John's Cathedral, the Town Hall and water mains. Overall 12% of the built-up area had already been lost. As the capital of the General Governorate put in place by the Nazis was Kraków, Warsaw found itself declared nothing more than a "county town". Far worse, it was one that would from then on be subject to unceasing and absolute terror: arrests random or orchestrated, street roundups, executions, and mass transports of people out of the city – as forced labour for the Reich or victims for the concentration camps. As early as in autumn 1939, the neighbouring forests and even the Parliament Gardens had already become places of execution, while December brought the mass murder of 107 people in suburban Wawer. The list of places of death and martyrdom also came to include Palmiry in the Kampinos Forest, the Kabacki Wood and Magdalenka, as well as the interrogation centre on Aleja Szucha and the Pawiak prison. The terror went hand in hand with a whole host of repressive ordinances concerning all spheres of public life. All notices, plaques and signs were to be in two languages, ration books were introduced, and curfews. Most Polish schools were simply shut down, and whole areas were designated for Germans only, as the city was divided into German, Polish and Jewish districts. The Ghetto that appeared in the latter as it was brutally walled off found itself closed from November 16th 1940. By this time it had somehow come to accommodate several hundred thousand Jews in an area of just 400 ha. The punishment for Poles seeking to help them in any way was death. From July 1942 onward, some 256,000 residents of the Ghetto were taken to the Treblinka death camp. But when the Occupiers finally sought to eliminate those who were left there en masse, the Ghetto Uprising of April 19th 1943 ensued. Fought with an intensity borne of desperation, its suppression could only be a matter of time, and it was followed by the Nazis' systematic levelling of everything that was left.

Tragedy followed tragedy, but Warsaw had also become the heart of the Underground Polish State, the HQ for plots against the Nazis and indeed the most significant centre of resistance anywhere in Occupied Europe. The Home Army was coordinated enough to launch both regular actions of small-scale sabotage (e.g. graffiti campaigns featuring the abbreviation "⚓" for Fighting Poland, "Hitler kaput", and the image of a tortoise – denoting that work for the Occupant should be carried out as slowly as possible), and more major diversionary attacks. Among the most spectacular of the latter to be perpetrated in Warsaw was the assassination of SS and police chief Franz Kutschera on February 1st 1944, as well as the so-called "Góral" action, whereby a sum of 105 million zloties was taken during a raid on a convoy from the Issuing Bank in August 1943.

Furthermore, the "above-ground" life regulated by the repressive dispositions of the Nazis was paralleled by a highly-organised "underground" existence in which there was education at all levels, conspiratorial theatrical performances and even sporting events. Hundreds of Warsaw-based underground publications were distributed nationwide, and a Delegate Office of the Polish Government in Exile (in London) continued to function.

On August 1st 1944, Commander-in-Chief of the Home Army, General Bór-Komorowski issued the order that began the Warsaw Uprising. Its aims were nothing less than the expulsion of the Germans from the city (and its protection from further destruction), its occupation by the Home Army under representatives of the true Polish Government, and the extraction from Stalin of a recognition that a sovereign Polish state had a right to exist. Going into battle with a heavily-armed and armoured German garrison 20,000 strong and able to call upon air support at any time were some 23,000 Polish soldiers, of which only 10% were armed, and backed up by just a 2-3-day supply of ammunition. But Warsaw's inhabitants swung behind the effort, with young and old alike helping in the fight and the building of barricades. Rescue groups were organized, medical posts, supplies of food and water. Uprising radio and postal services came into operation. Hearing of the action, Hitler ordered that every inhabitant was to be killed (no prisoners taken), while Warsaw was to be razed to the ground so that the whole of Europe might be given a terrifying demonstration of Nazi power. Hence, as consecutive districts were "pacified" in the first days of August, a terrible slaughter took place – in Wola district alone, some 40,000 citizens were murdered up to August 8th. Among them were the women and children acting as "human shields" against German tanks, and the wounded lying in makeshift hospitals – along with those tending to them. The fabric of the city was also burnt or otherwise destroyed systematically by artillery fire and bombing raids. Whole streets went down, often with their residents inside. Food was lacking, electricity, medicines and water, but the fighting for each street and each house was fierce. To finally put down the Uprising, the enemy had to order in frontline units of the 9th Army. Warsaw fought heroically for 63 days, mistakenly counting on help from the Red Army, which had come to a halt on the Praga side of the Vistula. With such slim possibilities for carrying on the fight, and in the face of the now tragic circumstances in which the civilian population found itself, the leaders of the Uprising decided upon surrender on October 2nd. Some 16,000 officers and men were taken prisoner, while the entire civilian population of 600,000 was now expelled – making this the greatest exodus in history up to that time.

The departing masses were directed first to a transit camp in Pruszków, from which they passed either to concentration camps, or else to forced labour in Germany. They left behind them almost 200,000 fallen or murdered Varsovians, including 15,000 soldiers, for whom the city ruins were to be the last resting place.

Back then, the poet Kazimierz Wierzyński wrote:

"And so it has happened! Just rubble now and disaster

And an inhuman yelping from far underground.

close her eyelids on the forehead stony

She dies defeated, dies victorious. (...)"

* Under an Ordinance of the Occupant dating from October 1939, Poles are to hand over all radio sets. The following year, megaphones nicknamed "barkers" by Varsovians appear on the streets, with a view to broadcasts of Nazi propaganda being inflicted on passers-by.

* The rationing system introduced straight away in 1939 results in 80% of the demand for food being by met by illegal trade – this despite the severest of punishments for those caught.

* The names of Warsaw's streets, squares, parks and bridges are Germanised in 1940: Piłsudski Square becomes Adolf Hitler Platz, Aleje Ujazdowskie – Siegesstrasse, and the Poniatowski Bridge the unoriginal Neue Brücke.

* On December 23rd 1940, General Władysław Sikorski honours the capital for its heroic defence by bestowing upon it Poland's highest military distinction, the Cross of the Virtuti Militari Order.

* The main means of urban transport during the Occupation are trams and trishaws, the buses and taxis having been requisitioned.

* In connection with the ban on practising sports and close-down of all sports clubs, Varsovians are forced to organise conspiratorial competitions such as this, the secret All-Warsaw Football Championships.

* The so-called Pabst Plan of February 1940 anticipatesthe establishment of a "new German city of Warsaw" and attendant reductions in area (from 140 to 15 km²), and population (from 1.3 million to 130,000).

* A 1942 vision of Warsaw from Nazi town planners, wherein the demolition of the Royal Castle precedes the erection of a great meeting hall, while the King Zygmunt III Column is to make way for a statue of the Germanic goddess of victory.

In the course of the Warsaw Uprising (1st August – 2nd October 1944):

* around 130 press titles and bulletins appear, while the Błyskawica radio station of the Uprisers is on the air uninterruptedly,

* the authorities of the Uprising bring back a Polish postal service run by scouts and delivering several thousand letters a day, in spite of the ongoing fighting,

* a moment for the Uprisers to catch their breath is afforded as artistes organise concerts in their honour – even in the Philharmonic Hall! In the first three weeks of August alone, there are some 35 such events,

* on the order of the Uprising Command, groups of film cameramen and reporters document the battle scenes and daily life of the city. The first chronicle gains a public airing at the "Palladium Cinema" on August 15th.

* On January 17th 1945, the so-called "Operation Warsaw" brings an end to the period of occupation of the capital by the Germans.

Nowy Świat Street in autumn 1939. As early as on September 1st 1939 – day one of the Second World War – Warsaw became a target for German bombing and bombardment that reached a peak on September 25th. In defending the city, the regular armed forces were joined by civilians acting under the direction of city president Stefan Starzyński.

The burnt Royal Castle, 1939. The aerial bombing and artillery bombardment of September 1939 did great damage to the city. The Royal Castle was burnt, and destruction was also wrought upon the heritage of the Old Town, along with St. John's Cathedral, the Philharmonic Hall, the Grand Theatre, the Treasury Building in Bankowy Square and most of the Warsaw palaces, as well as residential buildings and city infrastructure.

On the Poniatowski Bridge, September 1939. From the first month of the War on, Warsaw took in thousands of refugees from areas occupied by the German army, and later also people evacuated from Polish lands annexed to the Third Reich.

The Cemetery on Trzech Krzyży Square, 1939. The siege of Warsaw cost 6000 soldiers and 25,000 civilians their lives (with the number of injured or wounded exceeded 50,000). The fallen were interred in streets or squares converted into war cemeteries.

Adolf Hitler in Warsaw, 1939. October 5th 1939 saw the Führer (visible here as he crosses today's Piłsudski Square) take the salute at a parade of the German armed forces down Aleje Ujazdowskie.

Warsaw during the Occupation, 1940. From 4th December 1939 onwards, an Order of the Occupant requiring dual-language signposting was in force. Many places in Warsaw – including shops, cafes and even means of transport – were designated "Nur für Deutsche" ("For Germans Only").

The Ruins of the Warsaw Ghetto in 1945. As part of the effort to eliminate the Ghetto, the Germans carried its inhabitants off to the death camps. Once the Ghetto Uprising, which broke out on April 19th 1943, had been suppressed, this whole area of the city was levelled. In such a way, some 12% of the overall built-up area of Warsaw was annihilated.

A unit of Uprisers going into battle in Jasna Street, August 1944. August 1st 1944 brought the order from the Central Command of the Home Army that set the Warsaw Uprising in train. The most famous photoreporter during the Uprising was Sylwester Braun, alias "Kris". He made a permanent record of many dramatic and shocking scenes from the 63 days of heroic rebellion launched by inhabitants of Poland's capital city.

The Church of the Holy Cross aflame, August 23rd 1944. It was on this day that, thanks to a bold action on the part of a 250-strong unit of Uprisers, it proved possible to take the German Police Headquarters near Holy Cross Church. However, the Germans torched the church during the fighting, with the result that the towers, front and interiors were destroyed.

A "Thor" missile explodes in the Prudential Building, August 28th 1944. As early as August 1st 1944, the "Kiliński" Battalion of the Home Army had managed to hang the red and white Polish flag from the 16-storey Prudential Building on Napoleon Square. O August 28th, the Germans began shelling the square area with its heaviest railway guns – the explosion of one projectile destroyed this building which towered over the then city.

A column of German prisoners in Jasna Street, September 2nd 1944. Following the bombardment of the Uprising Central Command based at the PKO Building in Jasna Street, the Uprisers withdrew, taking the German soldiers they had earlier taken prisoner with them.

Szpitalna Street, September 4th 1944. The first days of September – the second month of the Uprising – saw the Germans engage in the heavy bombing and shelling of the northern part of Śródmieście district. The buildings of many city-centre streets were destroyed.

Crossing of Aleje Jerozolimskie, September 1944. To improve communications between the northern and southern parts of Śródmieście district (which was also possible via the sewers), an excavation appeared beside the barricades between houses numbers 17 and 22 on Aleje Jerozolimskie. Thanks to it, Uprisers and civilians were able to evacuate the parts of the city the Germans had occupied.

Taking water from a bomb crater in Złota Street, September 1944. The daily life in the fighting city was one of conditions difficult to imagine. Nevertheless the civilian population mostly supported the Home Army's soldiers in the first period of the Uprising.

A cemetery in the yard between Jasna and Mazowiecka Streets, August-September 1944. The Warsaw Uprising cost the lives of some 200,000 people, including around 16,000 soldiers. So, once again, Warsaw's streets, squares and yards became cemeteries.

The exodus of October 1944. After 63 days of struggle the Uprisers gave themselves up on October 2nd 1944. Those still alive at this point were expelled from the city – over 600,000 people passed to the transit camp in Pruszków.

reconstructed and modern

When hostilities finally ended in January 1945, inhabitants started to return to Warsaw. They were not deterred by either the ruined bridges over the Vistula or the mountains of rubble that lay where the streets had once been. Even in 1946, the American photoreporter John Vachon was able to report that "Warsaw is so complerely wrecked, and all gone, (...). You can hardly get an idea of what it must have been like from just miles and miles of bricks and skeletons of buildings. (...). The idea of its being a great city really comes across to you through seeing the people here. (...). Wherewer you walk here it is hunks of buildings standing up without roofs or much sides, and people living in them."

In the first months of 1945, a city deprived of water, electricity, means of transport and above all places to live was returned to by an average of 2500 people a day. By the end of the year 474,000 inhabitants were back in the capital.

At the time the Uprisers surrendered, some 50% of Warsaw's pre-War buildings were still standing, if variously devastated or damaged. The Nazis could not tolerate such a state of affairs, so special units devoted the last three months of the Occupation to the systematic blowing-up and/or burning of whole districts. Heritage buildings were particular targets, along with the city's technical and industrial infrastructure. In this pre-meditated fashion, Warsaw lost 90% of its places of worship, 80% of its museums and theatres. Overall, only 34 of 957 listed buildings came through intact. The first tasks to be begun in 1945 were thus mine-clearance and the removal of rubble: more than 20 million m³ of the stuff was ultimately taken away.

February 1945 saw an Office for the Reconstruction of the Capital City established to coordinate all activity in this sphere. The lack of dwellings was the most acute problem, so the first years after the war were characterised by a rush to put up housing estates and indeed whole residential districts, e.g. Mariensztat (1948-49), Muranów (1948-52), Koło (1949-56), Praga I (1949-66) and the Marszałkowska Residential District, MDM (1951-52). Also of great importance was the modernization of the old transport routes crucial to planning what was almost a new city, as well as the laying out of new ones. The 7 km "East-West" Route (Trasa W-Z) appeared in the years 1947-49, along with its tunnel section under Castle Square and Miodowa Street, as well as the adjoining Śląsko-Dąbrowski Bridge. In turn, between 1948 and 1954, some of the buildings along Marszałkowska Street were bulldozed to allow for the street's widening, and the route was extended into Żoliborz. The city layout that had hitherto existed was changed even more once Plac Defilad had been demarcated in the very centre. Other utilitarian buildings to go up in this period were the Central Statistical Office (1948-53), Ministry of Agriculture (1951-55), Dziesięciolecia Stadium (1955) and of course the Palace of Culture and Science (1955), whose exotic architecture led to its being dubbed the "nightmare of a drunken cakemaker" by the poet Władysław Broniewski. For the dominant style of the buildings rising up after the War was of course Socialist Realism, whose monumentalism of form and type of decoration linked up with the architecture of the Soviet Union. At the same time, work was ongoing on the reconstruction of Warsaw's historic buildings. Among other things, the Old Town district was put back in place, with such attention to detail that the work was honoured by the 1980 entry of Warsaw's Old Town on UNESCO's World Heritage List. The main period of reconstruction ended around 1965.

One expression of the renown that Polish conservators and architects had won for themselves as they restored palaces, churches and monuments to their former splendour was Warsaw's 1996 receipt of the Premio Internazionale del Restauro international award.

As Warsaw was being rebuilt, it had dramatic events played out within it, just as elsewhere in the country. Society was trying to face down the communist system imposed upon Poland. Finding themselves imprisoned on Rakowiecka Street were many patriots, including former Uprisers and soldiers of the Home Army. Only with the events of October 1956, and the famous address given by Party First Secretary Władysław Gomułka (himself a former prisoner) did Poles gain some hope that the totalitarian system might be changed. Most of the political prisoners were freed, and Primate of Poland Stefan Wyszyński came back to the capital from his internment in the remote south-east. However, the "thaw" was to be shortlived. As early as in 1966,the efforts to celebrate 1000 years of a Christian Poland met with obstruction on the part of the authorities. Students were out on the streets of Warsaw once again in 1968, the aim being to protest against censorship and state-sponsored violence, as well as to seek to support detained colleagues. The protests were stamped on forcefully.

In the decade that followed, the December 1970 tragedy on the Baltic coast left the new First Secretary Edward Gierek with little choice but to make at least some gestures in the direction of the nation and its capital. Among other things, it was decided that the Royal Castle in Warsaw might be rebuilt. In turn, areas around the centre and on the margins of the city became building sites in the 1970s and 80s as housing estates rose up in Ursynów-Natolin, Stegny, Bródno, Bemowo, Lazurowa, Jelonki and other places. Transport routes of importance to the city's functioning also came into being, notably the Trasa Łazienkowska and Wisłostrada routes.

In 1980, Varsovians joined the strikes taking place across the country that were demanding the right to establish the Eastern Bloc's first independent trade union. "Solidarity" really did come into being! Over the 16 months of what became known as the "Carnival", Warsaw was second only to Gdańsk as a centre for the independent movement comprising both Polish workers and the intelligentsia. The imposition of martial law on December 13th 1981 was a shock for everyone, but did not signal an end to the battle for an independent Poland. Rather, 1982 brought huge demonstrations crossing Warsaw in a further demand for freedom. The autumn of 1984 seemed to bring the whole of Warsaw to the Church of St. Stanisław Kostka in Żoliborz, the place of burial for Father Jerzy Popiełuszko – chaplain

of "Solidarity" whose activities prompted his murder at the hands of functionaries from the Ministry of Internal Affairs. The "Round Table" talks and ultimate regaining of independence by Poland in 1989 released an optimism, enthusiasm and entrepreneurship so typical of Varsovians. A great many new firms were set up, the foreign capital absent for 50 years started to appear, and the face of Warsaw entered a period of rapid change. A new airport terminal at Okęcie came into operation in 1992, while the first section of the long-awaited underground railway (or Metro) started running trains in 1995. As a whole, the last decade of the 20th century saw the existing fabric of the city augmented by the high-rise office blocs that would house financial institutions and company representative offices, as well as by new shopping centres, public buildings and hotels (including the Puławska Finance Centre, Galeria Mokotów mall, Warsaw University Library, Supreme Court complex, Sheraton Hotel, Holland Park and Daewoo Tower). Alongside these modern buildings are others modelled on the architecture of the 19th century. A completely unique venture was the reconstruction of the northern facade of Theatre Square by way of the recreation of the Town Hall and St. Andrew's Church. Nevertheless, Warsaw is still a green city, and its old parks are accompanied by new green space like the Botanical Gardens of the Polish Academy of Sciences in Powsin. There is development in other spheres of the capital city's life too: in culture, science and the arts. Warsaw is the seat of famous schools, higher educational establishments and scientific institutes. A lack of censorship post 1989 has borne fruit in a mass of independent publishing houses, art galleries, clubs and associations.

However, if Warsaw is to fully discharge its duty as capital of a modern state, there will need to be a great deal more investment yet, a steady and coherent implementation of well-thought-out projects, and effective governance. The latest to take on responsibility for all this is Lech Kaczyński, who won a clear majority of the vote in the first ever direct elections for the post of President of Warsaw held in autumn 2002.

* As early as on May 3rd 1945, the National Museum opens an exhibition entitled Warszawa oskarża ("Warsaw accuses"), which offered stark testimony as to the destruction deliberately rained on the city and its cultural heritage by the Nazis.

* The first neon lights in post-War Warsaw are installed at the Wedel factory on November 13th 1945.

* January 1947 brings the screening of the country's first film made after the Second World War, entitled Zakazane piosenki ("Forbidden Songs"). It presents the fate of Warsaw in the years of the German occupation.

* On January 17th 1955, the Historical Museum of Warsaw opens its first permanent exhibition devoted to Warsaw's fate from the 10th century through to the present day.

* Also in 1955, Warsaw plays host to participants at the World Festival of Youth and Students.

* 1956 sees the number of Varsovians exceed a million.

* On October 24th 1956, a crowd several hundred thousand strong gives an enthusiastic welcome to the newly-elected First Secretary of the Party, Władysław Gomułka, who will bring an end to Poland's Stalinist era.

* Year in, year out, Warsaw plays host to important cultural events, such as the Warszawska Jesień ("Warsaw Autumn") International Festival of Contemporary Music (since 1956) and "Jazz Jamboree" (since 1958).

* "Supersam" is the capital's first supermarket, opened in June 1962.

* Celebrations of the 700th anniversary of the founding of Warsaw get underway on January 17th 1965.

* The International Poster Biennale in Warsaw has been organised since 1966 – no coincidence then that the world's first poster museum is opened in Wilanów in 1968.

* March 1968 brings a suspension of performances of Adam Mickiewicz's play Dziady ("Forefathers' Eve"), under the pretext that it contains anti-Soviet elements – the decision draws student strikes and protests that are put down brutally by the communists, who then unleash a campaign against Jews and the intelligentsia.

* At the initiative of the late Jerzy Waldorff, a Social Committee for Care of the Old Powązki Cemetery is called into being in 1974.

* During his first pilgrimage back to his homeland, Pope John Paul II celebrates mass in Victory Square on June 2nd 1979. He utters words now considered to have launched the historic changes in Poland that were later to sweep through the rest of Eastern and Central Europe: "Let Thy spirit descend and renew the face of the land. This land!".

* While holding a meeting in Warsaw, the Congress of Polish Culture is brutally interrupted by the communists' imposition of martial law on December 13th 1981, in violation of Poland's then constitution.

* 1987 sees the unveiling, before the Church of the Sisters of the Visitation, of a Monument to the Primate of the Millennium, Cardinal Stefan Wyszyński, who died on May 28th 1981.

* The mortal remains of last King of Poland, Stanisław August Poniatowski, are brought to Warsaw on December 14th 1989.

* After a 50-year interval, the Warsaw Securities Exchange starts trading again on April 15th 1991.

* 1996: Warsaw celebrates 400 years as Poland's capital city.

Central Warsaw in 1945. This photo of the part of Warsaw between Marszałkowska and Nowy Świat Streets perhaps best illustrates the monstrous dimensions of the destruction that the capital had undergone. 85% of the city had been affected overall, with total destruction in many areas.

A pontoon bridge over the Vistula in March 1945. A view from the Praga side of the ruins of left-bank Warsaw. As all the bridges over the Vistula had been blown up by the Germans, the communications between the two banks of the river were assured by temporary bridges and boats.

Krakowskie Przedmieście Street, February 1945. It was to a city in ruins deprived of water, electricity and means of communication that the first inhabitants began to return after January 17th 1945, once the city had passed into the hands of the Red Army and Polish First Army. By the end of the year the population had swelled to nearly half a million.

The Old Town Market Square in 1945. This photograph presents the northern side of the Square known as the "Dekert side". Though this was the best preserved part of the Market Square, it was still nothing more than the building facades that survived; the remainder having been burnt down. When rebuilding work commenced, it was with a view to the finished product serving as the seat of the Historical Museum of Warsaw.

Nowomiejska Street looking on to the Old Town Market Square in 1945. The commencement of work on rebuilding the Old Town took place as early as in April 1945, through the safeguarding and reinforcement of any surviving elevations, the removal of rubble from interiors and the inventorying of any elements of the architecture that had come through the War intact.

The ruins of St. John's Cathedral in 1945. The September 1944 battle for the Old Town resulted in the blowing up of the Cathedral by the Germans. The only part to survive was the Baryczkowska Chapel and the miraculous figure of Christ raised by the Uprisers. Rebuilding work on the Cathedral continued until 1956.

The brought-down Zygmunt III Column and ruins of the Royal Castle in 1945. Having been burnt
and plundered in September 1939, the Castle was mined and blown up by the Germans in December 1944.
It was only rebuilt 30 years later, and opened to visitors in October 1981. The reconstructed Zygmunt III Column
was restored to its place in Castle Square in 1949, however.

Marshal Józef Piłsudski Square, 1945. All that survived of the destroyed Saski Palace was one fragment of the colonnade including the Tomb of the Unknown Soldier. Of the statue of Prince Józef Poniatowski only the plinth was left. However, the latter monument was reconstructed post 1965 and now stands in front of the Radziwiłł Palace in Krakowskie Przedmieście Street.

Plac Trzech Krzyży – the view towards Aleje Ujazdowskie, 1945. 1944 brought destruction to much of the Square, together with St. Alexander's Church. Only some of the buildings were rebuilt after the War, including the Institute for the Deaf and Mute. The western side of the Square gained new buildings connected with the national administration, thereby closing off what had hitherto been the exit from Wspólna Street.

The collapsed columns of St. Alexander's Church in 1945. The church destroyed in the course of the Warsaw Uprising was rebuilt in the original Neo-Classical form conferred upon it by Christian Piotr Aigner at the beginning of the 19th century.

Nowogrodzka Street in 1946. This is how daily life in a ruined Warsaw looked at the beginning – the rebuilding of places to live became the most important problem for Varsovians.

"Pédicure, manicure... ", 1945. Warsaw trade immediately adjusted itself to the conditions in the city. Wherever one turned, makeshift shops and stalls had sprung up selling, not only the essentials of life, but also more "exclusive" services.

Part of the interior of the Church of the Visitation, 1945. Of the 77 churches that had existed in Warsaw pre-War, no fewer than 54 were destroyed in what was to follow. Among those lost was the Church of the Blessed Virgin Mary in the New Town, which had had Anna Mazowiecka as its 1411 founder.

The ruins of the Town Hall in Theatre Square, 1945/46. The burnt-out and ruined buildings of the northern side of the Square, including the Town Hall, were pulled down in the 1950s. The Nike Monument to the Heroes of Warsaw went up in its place. Now the old building on this side of Theatre Square has been re-created, while the Monument has been moved to the Trasa W-Z area.

The destroyed Kierbedź Bridge in 1945. This was one of the capital's most characteristic structures until it was blown up by the German army as it retreated out of right-bank Warsaw on September 13th 1944. However, it was on its surviving pillars that the new Śląsko-Dąbrowski Bridge – a part of Trasa W-Z (the "East-West Route") was erected in 1949.

The ruins of Praga – St. Florian's Church in 1945/46. The wartime activity did not do as much damage in Praga as in left-bank Warsaw, though some buildings, especially in the area around St. Florian's, were destroyed, with 89% of the fabric there having been devastated.

A service at the Pawiak Prison, 1946. During the Occupation, some 100,000 political prisoners passed through the Gestapo's Pawiak Prison. Around 37,000 of these were shot, while 60,000 passed to the concentration camps. Part of the building was reconstructed and the Pawiak Prison Museum opened there in 1965.

The junction of Bracka Street and Aleje Jerozolimskie, 1946. This view is of the destroyed buildings of Aleje Jerozolimskie in the direction of Marszałkowska Street – one of the busiest parts of Warsaw's central Śródmieście district. Here it is seen in the first post-War years, just before rebuilding from scratch began.

A rail line designed to take away rubble from around 1946. The result of sappers' work was the taking away or disposal of 14,000 mines, more than 60,000 artillery shells, 6300 dropped bombs and 45 tonnes of explosives. More than 20 million m^3 of rubble were taken away.

Rubble-removal operations in the city, 1946. The years 1945-51 saw the Warsaw Office for the Reconstruction of the Capital City in action where all matters of the rebuilding of Warsaw were concerned. The slogan Cały naród buduje swoją stolicę ("The whole nation is rebuilding its capital") was meant to motivate more than just Varsovians to get down to work.

The reconstruction of the Old Town Market Square in 1953. The reconstruction and renovation of the Old Town lasted between 1945 and 1964 (the Square itself was completed in 1953), and constituted an example without precedent in Europe as regards the reconstruction of a whole city heritage complex in its configuration from several centuries before. In recognition of this, in 1980 the Old Town was entered on the UNESCO List of World Heritage Sites.

A View of Mariensztat, 1949. Warsaw's first post-War housing estate went up in the Mariensztat area in the years 1948-9, in connection with the construction of the nearby Trasa W-Z ("East-West Route").

The Palace of Culture and Science under construction. The 24-hectare Plac Defilad ("Parade Square"), with the Palace in the middle of it, was created by demolishing the greater part of the surviving construction along seven streets, and by levelling more than 100 homes. The Palace was a "gift" imposed upon a capital in the middle of rebuilding by Joseph Stalin.

Marszałkowska Dzielnica Mieszkaniowa ("The Marszałkowska Residential District"), 1954.
MDM – one of the foremost pieces of Socialist Realist design work, appeared in the years 1950-52 following
the demolition of part of the historic building of Śródmieście district. The appearance of the new district
was as different as could be from the unique character of the pre-War Marszałkowska Street.

"Wine lets thought take flight", 1949. This photograph shows a shop interior that well characterises the particular mood of those years. The advertising slogans represent some kind of propaganda that mobilizes clients to make purchases.

Warsaw "Mermaids"..., 1955. Under the eye of the Mermaid of Warsaw on Wybrzeże Kościuszkowskie, a presentation of the first examples of the Syrena 100 model of car (the word means "Mermaid"). The car was designed by the engineers at the FSO Car Factory in Żerań.

Aleje Jerozolimskie, 1965. A view of the northern side of Aleje Jerozolimskie between Krucza and Nowy Świat Streets – a bustling commercial centre of 1960s Warsaw. On the left is CDT – then one of Poland's largest department stores.

The "Eastern Wall" in Marszałkowska Street at the beginning of the 1970s. In the 1960s, a complex of residential and office buildings went up on the eastern side of Marszałkowska Street between Aleje Jerozolimskie and Świętokrzyska Street. The Pasaż Śródmiejski set out between the houses became one of the most popular places in Warsaw.

The Old Town Market Square in 1996. The rebuilt tenement houses of the "Dekert Side" of the Square are joined by three on Nowomiejska Street in housing the Historical Museum of Warsaw which has been in existence since 1948. This is the most important institution charged with the assembly, creation and presentation of collections concerning the history of the city. The first permanent display entitled "7 centuries of Warsaw" was opened to the public on January 17th 1955. To date some 470 temporary exhibitions have also been put on here

The Historical Museum of Warsaw – part of what was on display in 1998. Eleven tenement houses with a total exhibiting space of 4652 m² preserve valuable collections of Varsoviana: pictures, drawings, plans and maps, photographs, coins, the output of Warsaw trades and objects from history. The most interesting exhibits can be looked at in 60 exhibition rooms.

The Fryderyk Chopin Monument in Łazienki Park. The Secessionist-style Chopin Monument designed by Wacław Szymanowski was unveiled in Łazienki in 1926. Blown up by the Nazis in the course of the Occupation, it was reconstructed in 1958.

The Palace on the Island in Łazienki Park. It was on the site of the Baroque bath-house of Marshal Lubomirski that the last King of Poland, Stanisław August Poniatowski, built a palace that is a fine example of Polish Neo-Classicism. The Palace-Garden complex in Łazienki also includes other buildings worth seeing like the "White House", the Myślewicki Palace, the Theatre on the Island and the Old Orangery.

Wilanów Palace. This Baroque-style palace was erected in the years 1677-96 by King Jan III Sobieski, with a view to it serving as a summer residence. It was remodelled by successive owners. With its ornate decor and recreated royal apartments, it is located amidst picturesque gardens and a landscaped park.

The Saski Garden and Tomb of the Unknown Soldier. All that remains of the old palace of Poland's Saxon Kings are these three central arcades that had held the Tomb of the Unknown Soldier since 1925. The Tomb is surrounded by the tall trees of the Saski Garden, an enclave of green space in the middle of Warsaw.

Piwna Street. This longest of the Old Town streets links Castle Square with Wąski Dunaj Street.
To be made out in the background are the towers of the Pauline Church of the Holy Ghost from which
the Warsaw Foot Pilgrimage to Częstochowa's Jasna Góra has departed annually since 1711.

A View from Castle Square towards Krakowskie Przedmieście Street. It was from Castle Square
via Krakowskie Przedmieście and Nowy Świat Streets as well as Aleje Ujazdowskie that the Royal Way linking
the Castle with the Belvedere Palace and ultimately Wilanów ran. Passing this way today, it is still possible
to admire many palaces, churches and monuments, in fact some of Warsaw's finest architectural heritage.

A gathering in front of the Church of St. Stanisław Kostka, 1991. It was in front of this church in Żoliborz, where Solidarity chaplain Father Jerzy Popiełuszko is buried, that the greatest displays of patriotism began to take place from the mid 1980s.

The Monument to the Fallen and Murdered in the East, Muranowska Street. This recalls the martyrdom and deaths of Poles sent deep into Russia following the Soviet invasion of the Eastern Lands in September 1939. The work of Mirosław Maksymilian Biskupski was unveiled and dedicated as recently as on September 17th 1995.

A view of the centre of Warsaw. No longer does the Palace of Culture and Science hold absolute sway over Warsaw – newly-erected high-rise buildings of several tens of storeys are changing the face of the city as each year passes.

The Świętokrzyski Bridge. Warsaw has recently gained two new bridges: the Świętokrzyski Bridge in the central part of the city was given over for use in autumn 2000, while the Siekierkowski Bridge, linking the southern districts of the city either side of the river, followed in 2002.

Photos:

The Historical Museum of Warsaw:

Rembrandt Photographic Studios (p. 10)
Stanisław Nofok-Sowiński (p. 18)
Henryk Poddębski (p. 21, 22, 26, 28, 30, 31)
Franciszek Gazda (p. 24)
Zofia Chomętowska (p. 27, 29, 57, 59, 65, 67, 69, 71, 73, 74)
Julien Bryan (p. 38)
Leonard Jabrzemski (p. 42, 61, 72, 76)
Sylwester Braun alias "Kris" (p. 43-51, 58, 60, 62-64)
Edward Falkowski (p. 66)
Leonard Sempoliński (p. 68)
Alfred Funkiewicz (p. 70, 75, 77-81)
Teodor Hermańczyk (p. 82, 83)
Ewald Pawlak (p. 85).

Christian Parma (p. 84, 86-95)

Text and selection of photographs:
Anna Kotańska
Anna Topolska

Layout:
Aneta Stankiewicz

Translation:
James Richards

Publisher:
Wydawnictwo Parma Press
05-270 Marki, ul. Piłsudskiego 189 b
+ 48 22/ 781 16 48, 781 16 49, 781 12 31
e-mail: wydawnictwo@parmapress. com.pl
http://www.parmapress.com.pl

Printing and finishing:
DRUK-INTRO S.A.

ISBN 83-89157-40-3

© Copyright by Wydawnictwo PARMA® PRESS

Warsaw, Marki 2004